My Mom Eats Tofu

Written by Robyn Ringgold
Illustrated by Vidya Vasudevan

Edited by Catherine Chu
and Elyse Tadich

Solar Publishing

www.solarpub.com

Solar Publishing's Mission

To enlighten the lives of children and families through media that instills a sense of connection to nature and humanity. Solar Publishing promotes cultural awareness and publishes works that uplift and inspire individuals to live in harmony with themselves, the planet and its inhabitants.

Published by Solar Publishing
PO Box 2116
Ellicott City, Maryland 21041
www.solarpub.com

Text Copyright © 2009 by Robyn Ringgold
Illustrations Copyright © 2009 by Vidya Vasudevan

All Rights Reserved
No part of this book may be reproduced, stored in a retrieval system or transmitted in any form or by any means, electronic, mechanical, photocopying, recording, scanning or otherwise, without permission in writing from the publisher.

ISBN 10: 0-9785326-2-7
ISBN 13: 978-0-9785326-2-8

For more information about our books, and the authors and artists who create them, visit our website: www.solarpub.com

My Mom Eats Tofu is printed on 100% recycled paper.

Printed in the U.S.

This book is dedicated to:

Owna Camille Cordes
"The Last Unicorn"
1938 - 2007
~ Robyn

My parents, and their gifts to me.
~ Vidya

My friends all know about my mom
She saves bugs and hugs trees
She won't eat anything from animals
Not even from bees!

I invited my friend June
To spend the night
But would she think we were weird?
Would she not eat a bite?

I told June we were vegan
Before she came
We eat more than just tofu
No matter what some people may claim!

We start our mornings with granola
Mixed with nuts and berries
Then we pour in delicious milk
From rice or almonds but never dairy
We mix a super healthy "green shake"
Of kale, carrots, ginger and beets
When we drink it all
We get dried banana & mango treats!

At dinner Mom cooks grains
They taste quite nice
Quinoa, couscous, millet
And my favorite, brown rice!
We eat tasty veggies like brussel sprouts
Or beets and dandelion greens
And I always love adzuki, mung
Lentil and garbanzo beans!

We even eat veggies
That come from the sea
Nori, kelp, dulse
Are as tasty as can be!
Even though it may sound strange
To eat seaweed
It gives us the iodine and iron
That strong bodies need!

Mom grows herbs
And spices of all kinds
Like lemongrass, basil
Rosemary and thyme
Mom is quite the chef
She makes tasty meals
With turmeric, curry, cloves
And other herbs that heal!

There are some foods
That I just don't care for
But when we have sizzling lentil burgers
I always ask for more!
Some of my other favorites are seitan, falafel
Carrot tuna and raw kale
Raw foods are alive and fresh
They are never stale!

Mom says to eat all of our food
We should never waste
Lots of kids are hungry
They'd be grateful for a small taste
When we're done we throw our scraps
Into our composting bin
In the spring we use our compost
To make the soil strong and healthy again!

On weekends we go shopping
To the farmer's market outdoors
We carry reusable bags
And use them at different stores
We buy local fruits and veggies
That are freshly picked and in season
Local foods are Earth-friendly
That is Mom's reason!

Mom is a member
Of the local co-op
We volunteer for a few hours a week
And receive a discount when we shop

Our neighborhood garden
Was once full of weeds
But now we can play there
And plant our favorite seeds!

Mom prepares vegan cookies
Lots of pies and cakes
She never uses eggs or sugar
Just flaxseed and agave nectar when she bakes!
It's really fun when we dress up
We eat other countries' popular sweets
Like Halwa from India
Made with carrots, ginger, or beets

When I finished telling June
I worried she'd be scared away
But she was so excited
She couldn't wait to stay!

While June was at our house
Mom made hot dogs of tofu
And June enjoyed sharing
In all the Earth-friendly things we do!

June and I had lots of fun
Outside in the sunny weather
We plan to go on a nature walk
And hug trees the next time we're together
When it was time for June to leave, she said,
"Thanks so much, your Mom is cool!"
I said, "Thanks June!
I'll see you Monday at school."

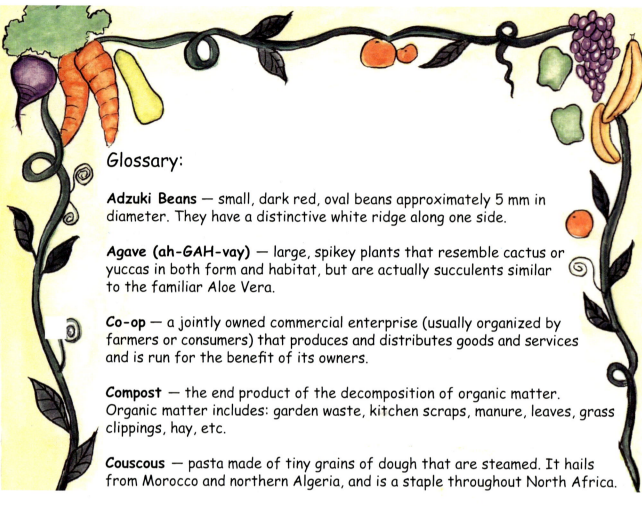

Glossary:

Adzuki Beans — small, dark red, oval beans approximately 5 mm in diameter. They have a distinctive white ridge along one side.

Agave (ah-GAH-vay) — large, spikey plants that resemble cactus or yuccas in both form and habitat, but are actually succulents similar to the familiar Aloe Vera.

Co-op — a jointly owned commercial enterprise (usually organized by farmers or consumers) that produces and distributes goods and services and is run for the benefit of its owners.

Compost — the end product of the decomposition of organic matter. Organic matter includes: garden waste, kitchen scraps, manure, leaves, grass clippings, hay, etc.

Couscous — pasta made of tiny grains of dough that are steamed. It hails from Morocco and northern Algeria, and is a staple throughout North Africa.

CSA (Community Supported Agriculture) — a membership based method of supporting farmers and getting fresh food regularly. Supporters of community agriculture share in part of the farmers' risk and pay in advance for a portion of the farmer's total crop. CSA members usually pick up fruit and vegetables on a weekly basis.

Dandelion Greens — the leaves of the common dandelion plant, which many people think of as a weed. Dandelions are edible and highly nutritious in both raw and cooked form.

Dulse — an edible algae harvested from the sea.

Falafel — a fried ball or patty made from spiced chickpeas and/or fava beans.

Farmer's Markets — markets, usually held outdoors, in public spaces, where farmers can sell produce to the public.

Flaxseed — a blue flowering plant that is grown on the Western Canadian Prairies for its oil rich seeds.

Garbanzo Beans — also known as Chickpeas, are a widely cultivated plant of the legume family, bearing pods containing pealike seeds.

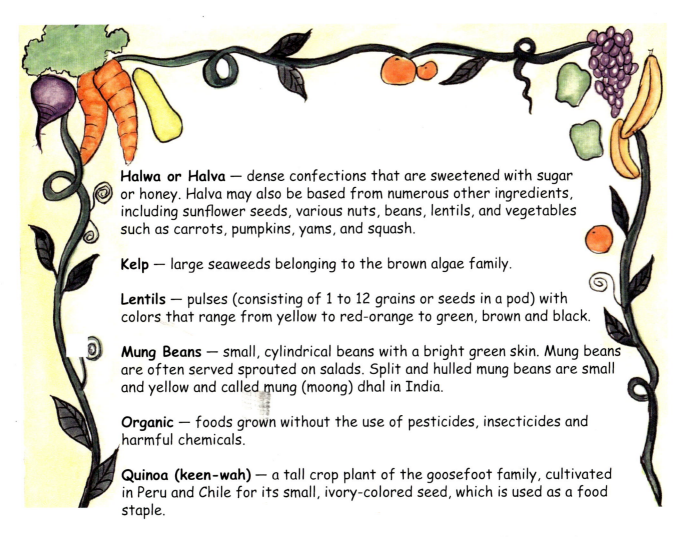

Halwa or Halva — dense confections that are sweetened with sugar or honey. Halva may also be based from numerous other ingredients, including sunflower seeds, various nuts, beans, lentils, and vegetables such as carrots, pumpkins, yams, and squash.

Kelp — large seaweeds belonging to the brown algae family.

Lentils — pulses (consisting of 1 to 12 grains or seeds in a pod) with colors that range from yellow to red-orange to green, brown and black.

Mung Beans — small, cylindrical beans with a bright green skin. Mung beans are often served sprouted on salads. Split and hulled mung beans are small and yellow and called mung (moong) dhal in India.

Organic — foods grown without the use of pesticides, insecticides and harmful chemicals.

Quinoa (keen-wah) — a tall crop plant of the goosefoot family, cultivated in Peru and Chile for its small, ivory-colored seed, which is used as a food staple.

Nori — a seaweed having a mildly sweet, salty taste, usually dried, often used in Japanese cookery as a wrap for sushi.

(Edible) Seaweed — any plant or plants growing in the ocean eaten for their nutritional value; includes some members of the red, brown and green algae.

Seitan — a food made from the gluten of wheat.

Tofu — food made by coagulating soy milk and then pressing the resulting curds into blocks.

Vegan — strict vegetarians who consume no animal products, neither do they use products derived from animals, like leather and honey.

Vegetarian — following a diet consisting of plant-based foods including fruits, vegetables, grains, nuts, and seeds, with or without dairy products and eggs. Types of vegetarians include lacto-vegetarians, ovo-vegetarians, and lacto-ovo vegetarians.

This glossary provides a basic description of the terms. Please do further research for information on nutritional value, benefits and preparation tips. Visit **www.solarpub.com** for recipes, activities & links!